# So You Have a Disease

# So You Have a Disease

DEVOTIONS AND STORIES TO RESTORE HOPE

## Beth Praed

CrossLink Publishing

CrossLink Publishing
1601 Mt. Rushmore Rd, STE 3288
Rapid City, SD 57702

Ordering Information:
Quantity sales. Special discounts are available on quantity purchases by corporations, associations, and others. For details, contact the "Special Sales Department" at the address above.

So You Have a Disease/Praed —1st ed.

ISBN 978-1-63357-320-8

Library of Congress Control Number: 2020935861

First edition: 10 9 8 7 6 5 4 3 2 1

# Contents

# Preface

My doctor says that I am dying. Every time that I see her, she tells me this fact in a new way. "The multiple sclerosis is killing you; You will not live a long life; your life will be shorter than most; the MS is causing your brain to resemble Swiss cheese; and you're lucky to know what you are dying from, most people don't."

She is a great doctor, and I truly believe that she is just trying to help me when she says these things. Maybe she thinks that I am in denial about my disease. I'm not. I just don't think that anyone can predict how long someone will live. What am I supposed to do? Just sit in a chair, watch television, and wait to die? All of us will die eventually. A perfectly healthy person can be walking along and be hit by a bus, while another person—to the surprise of his or her doctors—can live decades with cancer. The truth is, only God knows how long that I will live. I just don't think that He is finished with me yet and that is why I am still here. And the fact is that I have already died before this time. I had a Near-Death Experience (NDE) when I was just nine, and this experience was written about in Guideposts' *Mysterious Ways* magazine. It is also told again in this book.

The devotions in this book were given to me by God to help individuals when they are struggling to cope with a chronic illness or a disease. This is the only reason for this book to exist, and it was not written to make a ton of money. If my doctor is right with her diagnosis, I won't need money where I'm going. Money is not important to God. Why spend my final days on something that has little meaning? If God can use this sick, broken person to make a difference in the world, then that is everything to me, and my life has some purpose.

In this book, you will hear me repeat the same mantra: "Surround yourself with good people." There are many good people in this world. Find them and foster those friendships. We are here to help and support each other. You are not alone. Search for the good people out there—they do exist! If you feel alone, look around you and they will actually come running. God uses his children to help others again and again and again.

I also state throughout the book that maybe you are an "angel-in-training." Did you ever realize this? Maybe angels are developing from ordinary people who have gone through extraordinary circumstances, both good and terrible. Right now, you feel sick and discouraged. But perhaps God will use this to help you grow and develop into the person that He needs for you to be. How about this idea? Wouldn't that be incredible?

When I was a child, my grandfather used to tell me, "There are only two things that you have to do in life—die and pay taxes!" Well, he was wrong. There is one more thing, and that is to change. Our lives are constantly changing and I know mine certainly did in December 1995 when I developed multiple sclerosis.

Before that time, I was young; I was healthy; I was superwoman! Or so I thought. I worked long hours as a public relations executive for a Fortune 100 company in Atlanta. I was married with one child and another on the way. I also was completing my second master's degree in communications. I worked eight hours and then went to class at night. I was young! I was invincible!

Before I developed MS, I considered myself a spiritual person. I went to church on a regular basis. And most days, if I remembered, I prayed before bedtime. But, honestly, God was not a large part of my life. I knew He was there, but I was too busy with work, children, and school to take much notice.

It is interesting how an illness can change you. For some people, a chronic illness or disease can be devastating and more than they can handle. I realized just how unbearable illness can be while I was reading an Associated Press article about Dr.

Kevorkian, or Dr. Death. According to the article, twenty of the ninety-three people whose "suicides" he engineered had multiple sclerosis (MS)! Although multiple sclerosis can be a dreadful disease, most MS sufferers don't die from it. As I read the article, I was immediately struck by the power illness has to devastate people's lives. These gentle souls were so fatigued and tired of dealing with the MS every day, they no longer wanted to live—they wanted out.

I truly believe that people can sometimes have too much tragedy in their lives. Just like Dr. Kevorkian's patients, many of us can and do have more than we can bear. Life can be very difficult. Illness or disease greatly adds to that burden, and we can feel that we are broken. In reality, it might even feel worse than being broken. It can sometimes feel like our lives have been shattered. How do you begin to heal from your disease if you are in little pieces?

*So You Have a Disease: Devotions and Stories To Restore Hope* is intended to help bring God's hope and reassurance to individuals who feel like they are broken from illness. If you have been diagnosed with a disease, it will change your life. If I told you differently, I would not be telling the truth. Sometimes a disease can start suddenly, or sometimes you will slowly realize that something is wrong.

I hope and pray that this book is helpful to you. I would like to begin with a Gaelic blessing that is one of my mother's favorite prayers. Perhaps you have heard it before. Even though you and I might not ever meet, we are related. We are brothers and sisters. Not only because we all are suffering from a disease, but because we are children of God.

May the road rise *up to meet you.*
*May the wind be always at your back.*
*May the sun shine warm upon your face,*
*the rains fall soft upon your fields*
*and until we meet again,*
*may God hold you in the palm of His hand.*
—Gaelic Blessing

# Acknowledgments

**Katie Reitemeier**—you are a very dear friend who has always been there for me.

**Betty Alexander**—we have gone through everything together and you truly are a wonderful friend.

**Lynda Davis**—thank you for talking to me about my own dark night of the soul and for being there for me.

**Becky Fletcher**—you and I are lifelong friends.

**Ruth Schoff**—to the best counselor in the world who never judged me.

**Kari Beckwith**—to my incredible friend who I first met in a grocery parking lot.

**Cynthia Banner**—to the best neighbor that a person could ever find.

**Scott Praed**—my brother is always there to patiently help me and he never refuses to give assistance.

**Professor Leonard Teel**—to my journalism professor who taught me how to write.

**Hope F.**—thank you so much for working with me and recommending CrossLink.

**Phil Johnson**—thank you for visiting me those many times that I have been hospitalized from my MS and for being a terrific minister.

**Stacie P.**—my dear friend whom I miss spending time with since she moved out of state.

**Rochelle**—because of the hit and run accident, we went from being strangers to becoming good friends.

**Shawn Hansen**—thank you for helping clean my house when I couldn't.

**My late friend Jim Collins**—thank you for supporting me and helping me find happiness.

**Becky Ross**—Thank you for going on two memorable vacations with me to Florida and Hawaii and for being my friend for over thirty years.

**Dona Faircloth**—Thanks for sticking with me all of these years and for being such a fantastic friend.

**Aunt Mary**, **Uncle George**, **Aunt Verna** and **Cousin Sherry**—To the best relatives that someone could ever need. So grateful to you!

# The "I" Prayer Versus the "Me" Prayer

Never in my life have I ever seen God's presence so strongly. I was teaching as a music teacher for special education students when I was diagnosed with multiple sclerosis. My disease had an aggressive onslaught. It started out with seizures, then problems with walking and severe fatigue. I was finally diagnosed when I went blind in one eye for the first time. I eventually even lost my ability to play the piano or drive a car using my feet.

For numerous years, I walked with a cane to help me get around. But then I woke up and was paralyzed in my left leg. After spending three months in the hospital, rehab, and even a nursing home, I was able to go home with a walker. Never again could I walk again with just a cane. I wondered, *How much longer do I have left before this disease gets me and I end up in a nursing home permanently? And how much time do I have left on this Earth?*

I was angry at God and prayed a lot of "me" prayers. *Why me? Why have You let this happen to me? Why are You letting me suffer? Don't You love me? Why aren't You helping me?* The list went on and on. Finally, I said a different prayer: *It is obvious that this disease is not going anywhere, so how can I use it to help You, Lord?*

*How can I help You,* I had prayed. That's just the prayer that God wanted to hear! And boy, did I get an answer.

That night, I had a dream. I call it my "field dream." I was sitting in a field and a man in a robe walked out to talk to me. Sometimes, I wonder who he was. People ask me if he looked like Jesus. No, he was actually balding and a little overweight. Sometimes, I think he was an angel. But if he was an angel, he was not your regular, kind, supportive angel. I think he must have been some sort of angel-in-training. (That's the kind of angel that I would get. And honestly, he needed a little work on his angel abilities!)

He said that he wanted me to write a book on MS and that he would give it to me in a series of dreams. I must say, he wasn't very nice about it. When he told me, I bucked it.

*I can't do that, I'm working full-time*, I said.

*Get started*, he said.

*But, I can't*, I protested, *I have three children!*

*Get started*, he said again.

*BUT I'M SICK*, I practically yelled at him. *MS IS A MAJOR DISEASE.*

He turned to walk away and called over his shoulder in an off-hand way, *That's irrelevant.*

*IRRELEVANT! IT'S NOT TO ME!* I yelled.

*Get started*, he answered as he left.

The next morning, I thought about the dream. *Wow, that was some whacko dream that you had!* I told myself. *The men in the white jackets are probably going to come and get you any minute now!* And then I went on about my business, getting the children ready for daycare and going to work.

For months, I tried to forget the book. But God didn't forget. Each night, He reminded me of my promise—gently! I've never had problems with insomnia, but each night I walked the floor. I would get up at 5:30 a.m., take the children to daycare, work a full day, fix dinner, get the children finally to sleep and dishes done by 10:00. And then I would pace back and forth. I would wander the house until I would finally fall asleep by 2:00 a.m. Then I would start the process over again the next day. I was exhausted!

For three months, I refused to write the book. But each night as I slept, the book was writing itself. In my dreams, I could see the words on a computer screen as I was typing. Then, I would think about what I had dreamt as I drove to work. *What's going on with this book, God? I don't have time to write a book! It would never be published anyway. It's ridiculous! I won't do it!*

Finally, late one evening, I was walking the floor yet again when I knew what had to be done. "Okay, I'll write it," I sighed in tired resignation. *Just let me sleep.*

For the next eight months, I couldn't write fast enough. With each morning, there was more to write. I would go about my regular daily routine and then begin writing late at night. I finished the book on Thanksgiving Day and then panicked. *What if I had wasted all that time? What if the book was never published?*

That night, I said a prayer: *Okay, God, this is Your book! Show me who You want to have it!* Now, I had previously researched who might want *Multiple Sclerosis: Q&A*. I had researched small publishers, medium-sized publishers, and very large publishers—companies who were known to return manuscripts unopened!

The next day, one publisher's name was in my head, one of the largest—Penguin Publishing. I sighed, *I don't even have an agent, God! You don't want much, do You?* I took the manuscript to FedEx and said a prayer. I even kissed the package (which caused a few strange looks from the FedEx lady). That was on Friday.

The following Tuesday afternoon, I had just returned from work and was doing dishes when the phone rang. It was Penguin. They wanted the book.

Incredible, isn't it? But that's not the end for the story. For six years, *Multiple Sclerosis: Q&A* was the number one book on MS on Amazon! But really, I shouldn't have been surprised. It isn't my book. All I did was type it down. It is God's book. Do you think God would settle for anything less than number one for His book? I even wrote in the dedication, "To my sweet Savior who gave me this book in a dream."

In a lucid moment, my dear dad who had dementia stated it beautifully: "I really think you are getting spiritual guidance," he said.

"Thanks, I do too, Pops," I answered. "Why do you think this?"

"Well," he answered me, "you can't write that good."

My dad was absolutely correct. I can't write that well. But I had a lot of help, didn't I? I didn't write the book on multiple sclerosis. God did. All I did was write it down.

Most of the time, it seems that God doesn't answer me. I spend my time asking what I should do and being unsure. Never in my life have I felt God's purpose so strongly. But really, it isn't about me. I was asking all of the wrong questions. *Why me?* wasn't the question that He wanted to hear. Finally, after years of crying, praying, and begging, I said, *What can I do to help You?* Then, I got an answer with the MS book!

Now again, I have received inspiration to write a book to bring hope to individuals who suffer from chronic illness or disease. I sure do know what it is like to have a horrible disease. My MS has robbed me of everything. Twenty-four years ago, before I developed MS, I exercised daily and even did kick boxing! You can't get much healthier than that for exercise agenda. But now I use a walker, drive with my hands, am partially blind in my right eye, can't use my left hand except for one finger, and I lost my ability to play the piano (which is a major tragedy for a music teacher). In many ways, I am a shell of the fit woman who I used to be.

The next time that you talk to God, say a different prayer. Instead of saying a "me" prayer, say an "I" prayer. Say, *What can I do to help You, Lord?*

I guarantee that you will get an answer.

# There Is Good News and There is *Good News*!

There is good news—it is a new year! And with each new year, science comes closer to curing our illnesses and diseases. Maybe this will be the year we will find a cure for Parkinson's, or multiple sclerosis, or lupus, or ALS, or arthritis, or cancer, or AIDS. Each year, we move a little bit closer to cures for these and many other serious diseases and chronic illnesses.

And there is *Good News*! The *Good News* is that you are not alone in this. God is here with you during this trial. He knows your pain and grieves with you. God is here today and every day, guiding you and giving you the strength to cope. He is also here to show you the ways in which He wants you to go with this. To grow and learn. To become an even better person and to use this difficulty to teach others. To teach them the love of God, of His strength and courage, of His determination through your example. There is hope!

*Why should I feel discouraged?*
*Why should the shadows fall?*
*Why should my heart feel lonely*
*and long for heaven and home?*
*When Jesus is my portion*
*a constant friend is he.*
*His eye is on the sparrow*
*and I know he watches me.*
*I sing because I'm happy,*
*I sing because I'm free.*

*His eye is on the sparrow*
*and I know he watches me.*
—African-American Spiritual

# The Paper

I love this Bible verse: "Do not be anxious about tomorrow, for tomorrow will be anxious for itself. Let the day's own troubles be sufficient for the day" (Matthew 6:34).

Many years ago, I discovered this verse while reading the Bible. It jumped out at me. I was going through a difficult time and was looking for answers on how to cope.

I was so drawn to the prayer, that I scribbled it on a piece of paper and taped it to the wall next to my bed. Each night, I would place my hand on it and say the prayer. After a while, I no longer said the prayer, but placed my hand on the paper as a reminder of God's presence in my life. The paper still exists, tucked away in my memory box, with the image of my palm pressed into the middle of the paper.

> *In the same way, the Spirit helps us in our weakness. We do not know what we ought to pray for, but the Spirit himself intercedes for us with groans that words cannot express* (Romans 26).

# Why Me, Lord?

I think this has been the biggest question for me since I developed MS. I couldn't understand how God could let something like this happen. Didn't He love me? Didn't He care about me? Hadn't I been a relatively good person?

Then a well-meaning person said, "God never gives you more than you can handle." I wanted to slap her silly. God hadn't given me this! He loves me. He would never want me to suffer.

Then there was a terrible accident that occurred to a parishioner at my former church. It was Father's Day. The family had been to church and had just arrived home. The father thought all the children had gone into the house and he was backing the van into the garage, when he ran over and killed his youngest son. The father was literally beside himself with grief and agony over this horrible accident.

I thought about this occurrence. Was it true that God never gives you more than you can handle? Did God really give the father this terrible accident? To have him run over his own son on Father's Day? After coming home from church? Really? What kind of a sick God would do something like that?

Someone I know has a theory on this. It's what is called the "land mine theory." According to this theory, there are land mines in the world. Some of them are natural land mines and others are set by mean-spirited people. Some land mines are hit unintentionally. Sometimes we are hurt; sometimes others are hurt. In the case of the man and his son, they hit a natural land mine. God didn't cause the terrible accident on Father's Day. It was an accident, and it just happened.

Land mines are a part of life. They are part of living in an imperfect world with free choice. If we didn't have free choice, we would be like little puppets with which God just played.

We've hit a natural land mine, you and I. It's nobody's fault. God didn't give us these terrible problems.

The question is no longer "Why me?" The questions are, "What now? What can I do with this that's positive? What can I learn? How can I become a better person through this experience? How can I use this situation to help others?"

> *I have said these things to you, that in me you may have peace. In the world, you will have tribulation. But take heart; I have overcome the world* (John 16:33).

# The Cane and the Kids' Movie

It was the first day of spring break. I had promised the children that we would go see the new kids' movie. They had been looking forward to it for weeks and were counting down the days.

But that morning, I woke up and could barely move my left leg. I crawled out of bed and called the doctor. My neighbor, Katie, watched the children, and I drove to the neurologist. They inserted an IV, gave me a dose of steroids, and then taped the needle down to my arm.

"We will leave this in for five days, and you'll have to come back for more steroids tomorrow," the nurse explained. "And, honey, you can barely walk. You need a cane."

I somehow made my way to the local drugstore and purchased my first cane. As I tried to adjust to using it, I almost became road kill as I wobbled my way out to my car.

When I arrived home, I told the children that we would need to postpone the movie. Their eyes were wide with horror. "But you promised, Mommy." They were right. I did. An hour later, I found myself sitting in a darkened theater with cartoons dancing across the screen. As the theme song blasted through speakers, I thought, *Okay God. I hope there is some special hall of fame in heaven for mothers who go beyond the call of duty.*

That was a difficult day, but I got through it. I look back on it now and actually smile. It was a moment in time, and I survived it.

> *Though he stumbles, he will not fall, for the Lord upholds him with his hand* (Psalm 37:24).

# I Want It Now!

I truly believe that telephones are child magnets. Once when my children were younger, I was on the phone, and my young son came into the kitchen. He wanted juice and he wanted it now. When I told him "just a minute," he began to tug on my arm until it was quite useless having a conversation.

Even as adults, we are very much like little children. We want something and we want it now. We want a cure for our illnesses. We want our children to be trouble free. We want an end to our financial woes. We want a miracle. Not tomorrow, but today. The Jewish prayer for the Day of Atonement says it well. This prayer is so human:

*O Merciful God, Who Answers the Poor, Answer Us,*
*O Merciful God, Who Answers the Lowly in Spirit, Answer Us,*
*O Merciful God, Who Answers the Broken of Heart, Answer Us,*
*O Merciful God, Answer Us.*
*O Merciful God, Have Compassion.*
*O Merciful God, Redeem.*
*O Merciful God, Save.*
*O Merciful God, Have Pity Upon Us,*
*Now,*
*Speedily,*
*And at a Near Time.*
—Jewish Prayer for the Day of Atonement

# Thank You for Sandra

To say that my cousin, Sandra, had a rough life would be an understatement. She married an abusive man who tried to kill her and their children. She left him and set out on a life filled with hardship. She often worked three jobs to make ends meet, and yet she never complained. If you asked her how things were going, she would answer that God was good to her. The one goal in her life was to someday have a house. She worked to support her children and someday achieve that goal.

And somehow, even with her busy schedule, she always found time for me. I was younger than Sandra, but she was always there on holidays and birthdays. She would bring gifts for everyone. She, who was the least able to afford it, never forgot anyone. Then I grew up and moved away. When I returned for visits, there she was. She always wanted to know when I was in town so she could see me.

Finally, Sandra got her house. In the same month that she moved in, she also developed cancer. But that didn't slow her down or dampen her spirits. She would go for her chemotherapy and then go back to work. I marveled at her strength. "I'm feeling fine," she'd say, but I didn't see how.

Then, one morning, my mother called to tell me that Sandra was in the hospital again. "It's not good," she said. "Her bodily functions are shutting down."

So I called Sandra. I planned on being optimistic on the phone. But when she answered, I'm ashamed to say that I burst into tears. I wasn't prepared to lose her. "I don't want you to die," I blurted out.

"Honey, everybody's got to die sometime. Don't worry about me. I'm going to a better place," she answered.

"I love you, Sandra," I whispered.

"I love you too, sweetie," was her reply.

She died two days later. She slipped into a coma and gently went to be with God. I drove back for her funeral. I was amazed by how many people had been touched by Sandra. One after another, they went to the microphone and told how she had changed their lives.

After the funeral, I started on my long drive back home. As I drove, I questioned God. *Why Sandra? Why had her life been so difficult?* And then something amazing happened. The day had been overcast and dreary, and at that exact moment, the clouds opened up and a rainbow zipped across the entire sky. It was incredibly beautiful. The most brilliant and colorful rainbow that I have ever seen.

I pulled over to the side of the road and got out of my car. As I stared in amazement, tears of joy began to run down my cheeks. "Angels! Look who's here!" God seemed to be saying, "It's Sandra! We've been waiting for you. Let us all rejoice!" It was only fitting that God should send a light show in celebration of a very special angel.

*For he will command his angels concerning you to guard you in all your ways* (Psalm 91:11).

# Being a Rock Star

I had a student named Stephen. Stephen was eight years old and handicapped. He was in a special education class at the school where I taught music. Stephen's head was misshapen. He had a disease that was expanding his head from the inside out. Someday, it might kill him.

But you wouldn't know it to be around Stephen. His brown eyes shown with a love for life. And he loved music. He adored it. Every day that I came in, he would sing a new song for me.

One day in music class, Stephen announced that he wanted to be a rock star when he grew up. Immediately, an image of perfect bodies swaying before a crowd of cheering fans flashed before me. Stephen would never be a rock star.

As I was driving home, I thought about Stephen's dream. I thought about how unfair life was and what a sweet boy he was. And then, it dawned on me—perhaps my idea of a rock star and Stephen's were not one in the same.

The next day, I went to a costume store and bought ten pretend, inflatable instruments. When I got to Stephen's class, I made an announcement. "Today, we are going to be rock stars." I gave Stephen a microphone (as head of the band, of course) and gave the other instruments to his classmates. Then, I turned on his favorite CD, and away we went. We were jamming. You never heard such beautiful music or saw a more enthusiastic crowd. And Stephen reached his dream. He was a rock star.

This is what we need to do with our own obstacles. One of my dreams has always been to visit the Grand Canyon. To ride a mule and experience the beauty of the canyon firsthand. But now, I don't have the strength and stamina for that kind of journey. And the heat would very quickly do me in. Then, I was reading an article in an issue of *Inside MS*. It was about how you could travel and still enjoy yourself. In this article was an idea about seeing the Grand Canyon by helicopter. I don't know about you, but that sounds more exciting than sitting on a mule! Much nicer and without the saddle sores.

That's what Stephen taught me. To not just assume that I can't do something now because I am ill. I may have to change my idea of what a rock star is, but I can still have the experience.

*You turned my wailing into dancing; you removed my sackcloth and clothed me with joy* (Psalm 30:11).

# Thank You for My Friends

I have some very good friends—take, for instance, my former neighbors, Shawn and Katie. We lived in a small set of townhouses. We joked that we lived in Peyton Place. Everyone knew what is going on with everyone else. In addition, we all had access to everyone else's home. We found it out by accident when one of our neighbors was locked out of her house. We found that our keys fit everyone's door. We literally were like one big family.

My friends know that I am proud. It isn't a virtue at all, but a hindrance. A few years ago, when I first started using a cane, I really needed help but would never ask. One day, Katie and Shawn and a few other women in our complex showed up at my door.

"We're going to clean your house tomorrow," they said. "Now, don't say no, because we can get in, remember." By telling me, they gave me time to take care of the things that I would be really embarrassed about, like a dirty toilet. The next day, when I came home from work, I couldn't believe my eyes. An army had been through my house. It was so clean, I didn't recognize it!

And then a year later, Shawn came to my rescue again. I was having company for the weekend. It was Thursday night, seven o'clock, and I was just starting to clean my house. I had worked all week and was exhausted. The doorbell rang and there was Shawn.

"I'm bored," she said. I immediately knew something was up.

"What do you mean, you're bored?" I said, holding a broom.

"Yes, I'm bored. What I really feel like doing is cleaning," she answered with a sly smirk.

"Oh no," I protested.

"Oh yes," she said, grabbing the broom and sweeping furiously. "Oh, I'm feeling much better already."

How lovely my friends are. They know I'm proud, but we work through my pride in a humorous way. I know they don't judge me on how dirty my house is. They love me for who I am. Shawn, Katie, and I are great friends. I tell them both to pick out the nursing home that we'll be in when we're old, because we'll certainly be there together.

> *Therefore encourage one another and build one another up, just as you are doing* (1 Thessalonians 5:11).

# The Blinds and Other Small Gifts

A few years ago, I had the worst MS exacerbation I have ever had. I woke up literally unable to walk. I was taken to the doctor and given intravenous injections of corticosteroids. Unfortunately, with a compromised immune system, I then developed bronchitis, which quickly turned to pneumonia. It was the sickest that I have ever been in my adult life. I was in and out of the hospital. I was placed on antibiotics, inhalers, and a nebulizer. I was so ill, I couldn't lift my head off of the pillow. I couldn't watch television or read. All I could do was to lie in bed and try to breathe.

As the days stretched into weeks, I began to feel that I would never recover. I felt myself losing the battle. I thought that the multiple sclerosis would kill me.

And then one day, I felt light filter across my face. I turned my head and looked at the blinds. The windows were open, and the blinds were down. The breeze was lightly blowing, and the blinds would ripple with light and air. And then for the next few hours, I watched the light show. It was amazing. I never knew that so many colors existed. Gray to white, to gold, to blue. And then many textures and colors in between. And as the blinds moved with God's hand, I realized that I would live. God had sent me His beauty to awaken my spirit and give me strength. It took me four months to be able to walk again, but God was there with me. Even during my darkest hour, He had not forgotten me. He used something as ordinary and unspectacular as a pair of blinds to create something of infinite beauty. This was His gift. The breeze caressing my cheek saying, "Don't be afraid. Everything will be all right. See what I have for you."

> *God is light, and there is no darkness in him at all* (John 1:5).

# The Day that I Saw Jesus—My Near-Death Experience

My near-death experience occurred when I was nine years old. A few days after my May birthday party, I became very ill with an extremely high fever. I was placed in the hospital, but the experts couldn't figure out what was going on. For over a week, I drifted in and out of consciousness. The hospital told my parents that I might die. Because religion was still allowed in the school in those days, my classmates were told to pray for me.

During a lucid moment, I said a prayer to God. I told Him, *I'm too sick. I'm ready to die now.* And I lost consciousness again.

Then, I had an extremely bad pain in my chest. If it had lasted longer, I would have screamed. But then it was gone, and I felt wonderful. I was surrounded by a golden light, and I realized how very easy it was to breathe.

After basking in the glow, my room began to fade into view. I was still lying in my bed. But in the upper right corner of the ceiling, a bright light appeared. It was very small, but began to grow larger and larger. As the light got closer, I could see that it was a man walking toward me.

Finally, after what seemed a long time, he arrived. He was wearing a brown robe and was floating in the air. He had brown hair, a beard, and the most incredible eyes that I had ever seen. He smiled at me, and I smiled back. Then he spoke to me, although we didn't speak with our voices. We spoke with our minds, and that seemed absolutely normal.

The man said, "Are you ready to die yet?"

Immediately, I said, "Oh no, don't you know? I'm still a little girl. I haven't even lived yet." I then looked away for a minute and thought to myself, *That's strange. You said that you were ready to die.*

I looked back at him, and he smiled again. He then said the most incredible thing and something that I would never forget. He said, "What have you done with your life?"

And then there is a part that I can't remember. I've thought a great deal about this. In my opinion, I think the man showed me some things that I could do for Him if I went back. And then, I think that I was given the choice of whether or not I wanted to go back.

(A small aside—I don't think that these things happened to me because I was special. I think of it as being like a grand ceremony when the millionth person crosses the bridge. When this happens, there is a giant celebration with balloons and fireworks. The millionth person gets to meet the head honcho and then gets a prize of some sort. In my case, I was the millionth person over the bridge. Jesus was the celebrity and the prize was the choice of whether to live or die.)

The next thing that I knew, the man was halfway gone. I was watching as the light got smaller and smaller. Then, after being unconscious for an undetermined amount of time, I was very much awake. I was standing in the middle of my bed, and the light in my bathroom seemed so very bright. I immediately reached over, picked up the phone, and dialed my mother.

She was shocked to hear my voice. "Beth, are you okay?"

I was very excited. "Mom, a man has been to see me and he asked me if I was ready to die."

Of course, my mother panicked to hear about an intruder and called the hospital.

Suddenly a flood of nurses rushed into the room. They flipped on the lights and began looking around frantically. They wanted to know what this man looked like. I told them, and their eyes got big. Then they wanted to know what he had said. I told them that he had asked if I was ready to die. I then told them his second question: "What have you done with your life?"

As a child, I didn't understand what was happening, but all of the nurses immediately froze in their movements while their eyes began to dart back and forth at each other in a knowing way.

The nurses then did additional blood work and took me for yet another X-ray. The next morning, a new flood of people began to arrive. This time, a few priests, ministers, and a pair of nuns came to talk to me. They were all armed with notepads, and they wanted to hear about the man in the brown robe.

After a few days, I was allowed to go home. The hospital had found that I had a very severe case of pneumonia.

I was still an invalid, and it took me another three months to fully recover. It was summer and each day, my parents would place me in a hammock under a tree. I think that they thought the fresh air would do me some good. One interesting fact: before my near-death experience, I had been very afraid of the dark. As soon as I got home, I wasn't afraid anymore. I would go upstairs in the darkness. I didn't even need a nightlight. I wasn't afraid of insects either.

About six months later, I went to talk to my mother about my experience. "You know, Mom, I think that I know who the man in the brown robe was," I said.

"Who?" my mom asked in surprise.

"It was Jesus," I said.

"I think so too," she replied.

When I tell the story about my near-death experience, people ask questions about my background. "Did you go to church a lot?" "Did your parents teach you a great deal about the Bible?" Actually, I had a pretty normal childhood. We went to church most Sundays. But really all that I knew spiritually was that Jesus was born on Christmas (when I got all those presents) and died on Easter. I also knew Noah had a boat with lots of animals and that Adam and Eve were two naked people who loved each other. But I didn't really know much more than those facts, and I wasn't bright enough to have made up a story like this one.

Now at age fifty-nine, my experience still affects me. I remind myself daily, "What have you done with your life today?" All of my actions, both large and small, are based on my answer to this question.

> *For everyone who lives and believes in me shall never die. Do you believe this (John 11:26)?*

# Our Fear of Death

Regardless of our circumstances, we all will eventually die. If you are wealthy, you can't buy your way out of it. You can't run fast enough to escape it. Even at the farthest ends of the Earth, you can't hide away from death.

So why are we so afraid of something we can't change? There is the fear of the unknown, a fear of pain, a fear of losing who we have become, and a fear of non-existence. Perhaps of little surprise, the fear of death is listed as one of the top fears that people have.

I don't think that God thinks of death in the same way that we do. He scratches His head in puzzlement and thinks, *Why are they so frightened? Of what are they afraid?*

God assures us that this is not the end. Our lives on Earth are just the beginning. We will live eternally in heaven through the love of Jesus Christ. God repeats this assurance over and over again so we may believe. I have included four Bible verses on His assurance of eternal life with this story. This is His promise to a fearful world:

1. *For God so loved the world, that he gave his only Son, that whoever believes in him should not perish but have eternal life* (John 3:16).
2. *Jesus said to her, "I am the resurrection and the life. Whoever believes in me, though he die, yet shall he live"* (John 11:25).
3. *Behold! I tell you a mystery. We shall not all sleep, but we shall all be changed, in a moment, in the twinkling of an eye, at the last trumpet. For the trumpet will sound, and the dead will be raised imperishable, and we shall be changed. For this perishable body must put on the imperishable, and the mortal*

*puts on immortality, then shall come to pass the saying that is written: "Death is swallowed up in victory"* (1 Corinthians 15:51-54).

4. *We are buried therefore with him by baptism into death, in order that, just as Christ was raised from the dead by the glory of the Father, we too might walk in newness of life* (Romans 6:4).

# Special Needs Children

There is a saying: "Special needs kids are born to special parents." Perhaps a more accurate saying should be, "God is teaching us how to become wonderful parents to a special needs child." If we become a parent who emulates the unconditional, complete love of Jesus, it is because He is showing us how to do it. It isn't easy; it isn't fun; and it sometimes requires a person to do what is nearly impossible. But with God's help, we can become really fantastic parents to this beautiful child. We can bring joy to our children, enforce in them that they are indeed "special" people, and that our love for them is so great that we absolutely adore them.

> *As he passed by, he saw a man blind from birth. As his disciples asked him, "Rabbi, who sinned, this man or his parents, that he was born blind?" Jesus answered them, "It was not that this man sinned, or his parents, but that the works of God might be displayed in him* (John 9:1-3).

# My Mother Is Ill

My mother is the strongest person that I have ever known. She is never ill and always provides support and encouragement to everyone around her. Then, a few years ago, she was in a terrible car accident. She survived it, eventually recovered, and it seemed that everything was okay.

But then, she began to have problems walking and also began having severe memory lapses. The doctors discovered that the accident had caused her to suffer from "water on the brain." The hospital tried to alleviate the pressure by removing some of the fluid. Unfortunately, the procedure didn't work and the doctors felt that there was nothing else that they could do that would make a difference.

Recently, I took the kids back to my childhood home to see my mother for her eightieth birthday. She smiled at me, but then turned to my fifteen-year-old son and said, "Who do we have here? Is he your son or your brother's son?" I was stunned. How could she not know her grandson? Where had that knowledge gone?

Then through testing, it was discovered that she had Alzheimer's' Disease. I know that this can be a possible diagnosis among the elderly, but it doesn't feel commonplace to me. This is a brand-new experience and one that I don't like. Sometimes it feels like the mother who I adore is already gone. Anticipating the end of the story causes a hole in my heart that is unrepairable.

Prayer for hope: Dear Lord, how can I watch this happen to my mother? I can't change it, so how can I cope with the knowledge that she won't survive this? Please give me the strength to cope with her Alzheimer's' Disease.

*Do not be anxious about anything, but in everything by prayer and supplication with thanksgiving let your requests be made known to God. And the peace of God, which surpasses all understanding, will guard your hearts and your minds in Christ Jesus* (Philippians 4:6-7).

# A Blind Man's Trust

I was in a crab-apple mood. My alarm clock hadn't gone off. I hadn't had time for breakfast, and then I was late for work. When I was getting out of my car, my leg caught on the dashboard and I ripped my pantyhose. To top everything off, the office coffee pot was broken. *Why does everything bad happen to me?* I pondered. At least I could walk over to the mall in downtown Atlanta to buy some lunch and a new pair of hose.

I was waiting on the street corner for the light to change when I noticed the man standing beside me. He had a white cane. I glanced quickly into his face, saw the characteristic white color of his pupils, and realized that he was blind. I began to think, *Why is someone like him standing on a street corner? He can't possibly cross by himself.* I was in a hurry. I paused for a moment and then I reluctantly said, "Do you need assistance?"

"Oh yes," he said. "Would you mind helping me cross the street?"

When the light changed, he held onto my arm as we slowly crossed the busy intersection. When we got to the other side, he thanked me and I started on my way. But then I stopped. *I know you're in a hurry, but you just can't leave him there!*

"Where do you need to go?" I asked him.

"To the mall," he answered me. Honestly, I was bugged as we walked the three blocks to the entrance. *What kind of emergency could there possibly be that would cause him to do something like this?* So, my curiosity got the best of me and I asked him, "What are you planning on doing at the mall?"

"It is my friend's birthday, and I want to get her a card," he told me.

And then I got really nosy and asked, "How can you come all the way to downtown Atlanta by yourself, and how were you planning on crossing the street?"

Then he told me, "When I get to the street corner, I begin to pray and ask God to send a good person to help me. I then just stand there and wait until He sends the person that He has chosen."

Suddenly, I felt very ashamed. *Was this self-serving individual really the good person that God had sent to help this blind man?* By this time, he and I had reached the mall.

I then stepped further outside my comfort zone and said, "Would you like for me to help you pick out a card?"

"Oh, could you? That would be wonderful!" he rejoiced. We then walked into the Hallmark store and began to look at cards. I looked a few over, described what was on the front cover, and read the inside sentiment to him. He chose the card with the birds on the front. He then dropped a twenty-dollar bill on the counter and waited for the cashier to hand him his change.

As we were walking back to the subway, I asked, "How do you know that she didn't rip you off?"

"I don't," he said. "I have found, however, that God has created many wonderful people, and I trust that He will continue to watch over me."

I swallowed hard and began to notice what a lovely day that it was. The sun was shining, the birds were singing, and it was a perfect day to take a walk with a friend. As I helped Frank onto the subway, I thanked him for spending time with me and then hurried back to the office.

When I strolled back into work, things were great. The coffee pot still wasn't working, I hadn't had lunch, and my co-worker pointed out that my hose were badly ripped.

"Oh yes, thank you." I nodded to her with a smile as I sat back down at my desk. But those things didn't bother me. Frank's trust in God was amazing and was far superior to mine. Spending an hour with him was uplifting to me. Frank saw what was really important in life and had trusted in God with an unfaltering faith.

Perhaps the person who was blind to God's graces had actually been me. So, God blessed me on that lovely day by giving me the privilege of spending an hour with Frank.

*Again Jesus spoke to them, saying, "I am the light of the world. Whoever follows me will not walk in darkness, but will have the light of life"* (John 8:12).

# Therefore, But by the Grace of God, Go I

One of my mother's favorite sayings is: "Therefore, but by the grace of God go I." This means—that could be me.

I realized the full extent of this saying when I was crossing a busy intersection in Atlanta. With the "walk" light, a handful of us began to cross. Suddenly, a car rounded the corner and hit the woman right in front of me. She flew over the top of the car and landed on the pavement. The woman who hit her stopped briefly, leaned out of her window, looked at the woman on the ground and said, "Are you okay?"

Because she hit her head, the confused victim nodded "yes," and the perpetrator sped away. Numerous people began running after the hit-and-run driver and yelling for her to stop. In the meantime, the victim rose to her feet.

"What are you doing? Get back down on the ground while we call an ambulance," I told her.

"No, I have to get to work," she said to me with a dazed expression.

"Okay, I'm going with you," I told her. When we got to her office, I told her co-workers that she had just been hit by a car. I ordered them, "Take her to a hospital. She is not okay," and left them with my contact information. The victim had multiple injuries. She had a concussion, broken ribs, and suffered permanent hearing loss. I was one of the individuals that testified in the court case against the hit-and-run driver.

If it had just been two seconds later, it would have been me who sailed over the car and landed on the concrete. It was just the luck of the draw. If I had been walking faster or if the car had been a little slower, things would be different.

We need to be grateful to God for everything that He has given to us. I am grateful that I had wonderful parents. I am grateful that I live in a safe place. I am grateful that I now use a walker to help me walk and hand controls on my car that allow me to drive.

As Christians, we can't be arrogant. We can't boast that we are so beautiful, so rich, so educated, or have the perfect children. Things happen. I could have a problem with alcoholism. I could have a mentally impaired child. I could be homeless. I could be hit by a car. Or I could be crippled by a terrible disease.

Prayer: Therefore by the grace of God, I will not judge others. I will remind myself to be grateful for all that I have and helpful to all of God's children who need assistance.

> *You judge according to the flesh; I judge no one* (John 8:15).

# The Unexpected Path

I am so sorry, my dear friend, that you are going through such a difficult time. I believe that God has a special way of dealing with horrendous situations. Sometimes, God will send a follower down Path A. This path is lovely with green trees and beautiful flowers. But then, he sends you down Path B. This is a horrible path full of rocks, sticks, trash, and thorn bushes. Soon, you are covered with scratches and bruises. You can't understand how a God who supposedly loves you could ever send you down this path. After what seems like an eternity, you round the corner to Path C. This new path is the ultimate in beauty. Soon, you realize that God wanted you to get to Path C all the time. The truth is you couldn't have reached Path C any other way. You couldn't fly, jump, or run. There is only one way to get there—down Path B.

You are going through a difficult spell, but God is watching over you. You are on Path B, and it hurts. But God knows your pain. He cares about you, and so does everyone who loves you. We will not desert you.

> *For your name's sake, O Lord, preserve my life: in your righteousness, bring me out of trouble* (Psalm 143:11).

# My Lack of Faith

I wrote this email to a friend of mine about a problem with faith that I was experiencing:

Wanted to share something with you about my faith. I already told you that for the first time in my life, my faith has been suffering. I am currently reading a very old, yellowed book that I have by C.S. Lewis, *Mere Christianity*. It is very difficult to absorb, so I am reading it very slowly. I only read one chapter a day so I can think about what Lewis has said.

Anyway, my current problem with faith revolves around two ideas. My first faulty conclusion is that some really terrible things have happened to me recently, that God isn't doing anything about them and is just letting me suffer; and so, God must not love me or care about me. My second faulty conclusion is that God does love me and wouldn't throw me under the bus, and because this is what is happening, there must not be a God at all. (But how can I even possibly think this? I saw God, after all, during my near-death experience, so what am I thinking?!)

But I think that there is a third conclusion. God does love me and doesn't want me to suffer. However, these problems are not something that can be resolved quickly. God does care about me and will help me, but it will take some time to do it. I need to trust that He will help me and be patient.

The third conclusion is the right one, and it is already happening. After a ton of work, it looks like the top two difficulties, of which I was most afraid, are going to be resolved.

I don't know how God puts up with me! My mother was right, I "think too much." Sometimes, I conclude my problem is that I have a very analytical mind that thinks through things logically. If people who have never seen God can believe in Him, what is my excuse for my doubts? I know that God forgives me for this too, but I am definitely one of His "high maintenance children." I'm not an easy child to love and need a ton of supervision on His end. I'm so glad that He doesn't give up on me.

Thanks for letting me share this problem that I was having with my faith.

> *He who did not spare his own Son but gave him up for us all, how will he not also with him graciously give us all things* (Romans 8:32)?

# Get Started

I keep having a strange dream. In it, I will be sitting in a field and a man walks toward me. It is always the same man. He is just an ordinary-looking individual, balding and a little overweight. He comes to talk to me. Our conversations are always the same. Usually, he wants me to do something and I refuse. Each time when he leaves, he calmly calls back to me over his shoulder: *Get started.*

How many times are we too busy to accept what God wants for us. We have our own problems, our own issues. *If I can work you into my busy schedule, Lord, I'll pray and we'll spend some quality time together. I can't right now, let me get through this first. After I have all my ducks in a row, after this has been worked out, then I'll help You with that situation.*

But the ducks are never in a row. Don't we ever realize that tomorrow never comes? The fact that we are too busy, or too stressed, or have little time, or even have a chronic disease is irrelevant. God doesn't want to be our little project that we will get to when we have time or when He is convenient for us.

What God asks of you will be difficult. It might not make sense. It might seem impossible. But today is the day. Now is the time. Get started.

> *Now what I am commanding you today is not too difficult for you or beyond your reach* (Deuteronomy 30:11).

# The Dog Biscuit Ornament

I left an abusive relationship at a run with only the clothes on my back. When I finally got my things from my home three months later, anything that I had of value had magically disappeared.

My first Christmas on my own was difficult. I had little money, no Christmas tree, and not a single ornament. So, I cut down a small evergreen tree from my yard. My daughter had brought a package of sparkles home from school. We took some dog biscuits, a little glue, and spent hours being creative. Before long, our tree was covered with sparkly biscuits. Now every Christmas, the very first ornament that I put on the tree is one of the dog biscuits that I saved.

You've heard the saying, "You can't take it with you." But most of our life, it seems, is spent on acquiring things that we don't need—those designer clothes, that fancy car, and the expensive house. Why do we spend so much of our time, energy, and money on things that really have no meaning?

Whenever I hang the dog biscuit on the Christmas tree, I remind myself that all of the things that I thought were important weren't important at all. As children of God, we don't need expensive, material items to have a meaningful life.

*For we brought nothing into the world, and we cannot take anything out of the world* (1 Timothy 6:7).

# Why Isn't God Answering My Prayer?

Sometimes it seems like God isn't answering our prayers. We pray and pray and pray. Despite our pleas, He doesn't answer us. We get angry. "Don't You care about me, God? Why aren't You helping me?" As a result, some individuals will even stop believing in a kind and loving God. We rationalize, *If He doesn't believe in me, then I won't believe in Him.*

But maybe the answer is not that simple. An even more possible solution to why God isn't answering us is that we are praying for the wrong things. You might pray that God will help make your job better and more tolerable. But God doesn't improve your situation, and you still hate going to work. Maybe God's solution is not fixing your job, but finding a new occupation for you. Maybe the reason why He isn't answering you is that you are praying the wrong prayer. Maybe He can't fix your job because this is not where you are meant to be.

Perhaps you pray that your disease will be cured. But maybe the cure is coming soon when a new discovery will be made. You and millions of other people will all be cured on that very special day. The cure for your arthritis, your Parkinson's disease, or your MS might be right around the corner. But it can't happen until the scientist that God has chosen will make it happen for you and many other people who are also suffering.

> *I wait for the Lord, my soul waits, and in His word I hope* (Psalm 130:5).

# The Miss America Pageant

When I was young, every year my family used to watch the "Miss America Pageant." We were always amazed by who was chosen as Miss America. Just within our family of five, we always chose at least three different winners among ourselves. If our small family couldn't agree on this smorgasbord of beautiful women, how could the judges?

According to God, we are "fearfully and wonderfully made." Everyone is beautiful in God's eyes, even those sick with a chronic illness. There will never be beauty pageants in heaven because everyone would be a winner there, including you.

> *Why, even the hairs of your head are all numbered.*
> *Fear not; you are of more value than many sparrows*
> (Luke 12:7).

# Hand Controls on My Car

I have had hand controls on my car for fifteen years now. My MS has robbed me of the feeling in my feet, so I can't use them to drive. Instead, there is a bar on the left side of the dashboard that I use as the gas and brake. Attached to the right side of the wheel is a small knob that allows me to steer the car with just one hand.

One day a young bagger was helping me put groceries in my car. I had two doors open, the door right behind the driver's side and my door. The bagger saw the hand controls and wondered what they were. I then told him. I explained how I used the bar and the knob. I showed him the foot guard that protects the gas and brake pedals from my unusable feet. I then explained that these accommodations allowed me to drive with my hands. The youthful man was silent for a moment and then exclaimed loudly, "Cool!"

Without this complicated device, I would be trapped and unable to leave my home. Now, I can drive down the street and no one even knows that I am handicapped. I can travel down the highway and even go out of state. I can go wherever I wish.

I had never thought of hand controls as cool, but he was right. Without a doubt, they are cool. I am so grateful that I have these accommodations that allow me to be independent!

*Now the Lord is the Spirit, and where the Spirit of the Lord is, there is freedom* (2 Corinthians 3:17)!

# Mourning the Death of a Friend

Three dear friends of mine died in the same week, and I was in a funk. Two of the individuals were elderly, so it was not entirely unexpected, but it still was difficult. My heart was heavy, and I felt myself just going through the motions of the day. It was if there had been some "Invasion of the Body Snatchers" real-life event and everyone that I had known was missing. In a moment of prayer, I whispered, "The world is so quiet. Where have you gone?"

When you love someone, a large amount of your time is spent with that person. You laugh together at the same things and share common experiences. You support each other when that job doesn't work out, when your daughter pushes your boundaries, or when everything "goes to hell in a hand basket."

When someone who I love dies, I think that the whole world should come to a screeching halt. Cars shouldn't move, and time should stand still. I always feel puzzled when traffic keeps moving at a brisk pace and my watch keeps ticking away the seconds. How can life keep going?

Prayer: Today, I will remember the good times that I had with my friend and how the world was improved by her presence. I know that she made my life better. I miss her. Dear God, bring comfort to my aching heart.

*Blessed are those who mourn, for they shall be comforted* (Matthew 5:4).

# When My Dog, Lady, Died

To say that I loved my dachshund, Lady, would be an understatement. Every night, Lady would sleep with me. She would turn around a few times, place her head on my shoulder, and fall asleep with a contented sign. She was also a mischievous dog who had a penchant for stealing food. One day, I had just finished cooking hot dogs and had placed my plate on the table. Remembering that I had forgotten the mustard, I stood up briefly to retrieve the bottle that was resting on the counter right behind me. When I turned around to eat my lunch, my hot dog was gone and the empty bun was just sitting there. Lady, of course, had disappeared and was enjoying a scrumptious hot dog while she hid under the bed.

Lady was only five when she developed leukemia. She wasn't acting like herself, and I took her to the vet on a Friday. After he did blood work, he told me that she was going to die and that I needed to "put her down." I was stunned and couldn't bring myself to do it. Instead, I believed that I could force her to take the prescribed medication and hoped for the best. By early Monday morning, I knew that I would have to take her back to the vet. Before I could arrange the appointment, Lady had a brief seizure and died.

I was devastated. I couldn't concentrate and was unhappy all the time. The weeks turned into months, and my grief still hadn't lessened. Then I was hit with another jolt. My MS had worsened and was attacking my brain. None of the medications were helping, and my doctor told me that the multiple sclerosis could eventually kill me. I felt lost and alone.

Then one night, I had a dream about Lady. I dreamt that I was walking along a path in a forest and Lady came dashing down the road toward me. When I could see that it was her, I sat down on the path. In her excitement, she began to jump up and down and tried to lick me on the face.

"Lady, Lady, I have missed you," I exclaimed. But then it dawned on me. "But you died, how can you be here with me?" I thought further and realized that I too must have died. I then said quietly to myself, "Oh, I see."

The two of us sat there for a long time, and I finally stood up. I ventured further down the path while she scampered behind me.

God had given me this dream for a reason. After that dream about Lady, my sadness was gone. I realized that the MS hadn't killed me yet and maybe God had more things for me to do. I also realized that I would see Lady again. Someday, she would be my companion for a second time. I knew that when I finally died, Lady would be the very first of God's creatures to greet me.

> For what happens to the children of man and what happens to the beasts is the same; as one dies, so dies the other. They all have the same breath, and man has no advantage over the beasts, for all is vanity. All go to one place. All are from the dust, and to dust all return. Who knows whether the spirit of man goes upward and the spirit of the beast goes down into the earth (Ecclesiastes 3:20-22)?

# Suffering from Mental Illness

I have this image of my daughter that sticks in my head. She is four years old and wearing her Sunday finest. An Easter bonnet frames her face, and she is gazing peacefully out the window. Fast forward to the reality of today—her hair is purple, she has multiple piercings, and she is constantly bringing home men who she has met online. I fear for her life and realize that someday it might be me who has to identify her body.

I grieve over the sweet, young woman who she used to be and this defiant stranger who lives in my home. Sometimes, I am afraid of her behavior.

It was a snowy day, and she wanted me to take her somewhere. When I told her that it wasn't safe to drive, she became outraged. She screamed at me. She said that she wanted me to die and burn in hell, all because I couldn't take her where she wanted to go.

My daughter suffers from Borderline Personality Disorder. It isn't her fault, and it isn't my fault. It just happened. The doctor says that it is a chemical problem in her brain. But I have to wonder if she inherited it. Genetically speaking, there was this elderly aunt who was known in the extended family as being a little odd and who needed constant family intervention.

As our bodies can become ill, so can our minds. Pray for God's kind guidance as your family battles this disorder. There is no disgrace in a family member having a mental illness. You are not to blame. It is what it is. Do not be ashamed.

*Casting all your anxieties on him, because he cares for you* (1 Peter 5:7).

# Unexpected Circumstances

In Lemony Snicket's book series, *A Series of Unfortunate Events*, things go from bad to worse for the characters who suffer from all sorts of terrible problems.

However, it sometimes can seem that we too are living in one of Mr. Snicket's stories. Unexpected and unforeseen events happen to even the most careful people. You are the safest driver in the world and always drive within the speed limit. And yet everything is changed when another car rounds the corner and plows into you. Your honor-student son unexpectedly commits suicide when his long-term girlfriend breaks up with him. Without warning, the company where you have worked your entire life goes out of business and you find yourself looking for another position at age fifty.

Although these things might seem out of the norm, perhaps the reality of it all is that unplanned events are a normal part of life. I read an article recently about the top ten worst college degrees. The worst degree was architecture. Who could have predicted that situation? I assume that there are numerous unemployed architects who are now working at fast-food restaurants. As I read the article further, I also discovered that both of my masters' degrees were also in the top ten. I had always thought that I would work forever as a music teacher. But then after only ten years, I developed multiple sclerosis and quickly lost my ability to play the piano. I then got another degree, went into journalism, and worked part-time at a local paper. With the development of the internet, information is now free. If they are still in business, newspapers are cutting their staff to just the minimum number of writers needed. So, journalism also turned out to be a bad field.

I never thought that I would develop a disease like MS, and I knew for certain that my feet would always be sufficient to take me wherever I wanted to go. That just wasn't the case.

Maybe you too have a disease or a chronic illness which won't seem to go away. Regardless of what unfortunate event might occur in your life, you aren't alone. You can always count on the love of Jesus to help you when you become disheartened and to give you courage to face any obstacle.

*Three times I pleaded with the Lord about this, that it should leave me. But He said to me, "My grace is sufficient for you, for my power is made perfect in weakness." Therefore I will boast all the more gladly of my weaknesses, so the power of Christ may rest upon me. For the sake of Christ, then, I am content with weaknesses, insults, hardships, persecutions, and calamities. For when I am weak, then I am strong* (2 Corinthians 12: 8-10).

# God's Alarm Bell—Stress

According to an article in WebMD, seventy-five to ninety percent of doctor visits are related to issues that have been made worse by stress. This is not a surprise to many people. I know that my MS is exacerbated by stress, and I don't think that it takes a rocket scientist to be able to predict what stress can do to a man with a heart condition.

I had a very stressful situation a few years ago. I sat down and made a list of twenty items about which were causing angst. Then a year later, I found the list in a drawer. For ten of the items, I was surprised to discover that I had either solved them or they had resolved on their own. Another five items were "still in the works," but progress was being made on fixing the issues. There were only five items that could basically be called unsolvable. So, I found that seventy-five percent of my out-of-control, stressful situations had been solved or could be fixed sometime in the near future.

I think that stress is actually God's alarm bell that He has given to help us. When the alarm bell goes off, it is His way of alerting us that something needs to be changed before we are harmed. Instead of feeling overwhelmed, we need to say a prayer and ask, "Okay, God, how can You and I fix this situation?"

*And which of you by being anxious can add a single hour to his span of life* (Matthew 6:27)*?*

# Uncertainty

It seems that my faith is at its lowest when I am uncertain about how something will turn out and when I am concerned about finding a possible solution. I will lose sleep worrying about it. At night, in the dark, I will pace back and forth through the house. The next day won't be any better either.

But why am I so worried? God is not going to throw me under the bus. He cares about me. God wants me to be happy and to have a good life. If I profess to being a Christian, I must believe that God is there for me. To be uncertain about my life also shows my concern that God can't help my situation.

What kind of a Christian am I? Do I believe in a God who helps save His followers?

*For I know the plans I have for you, declares the Lord, plans for welfare and not for evil, to give you a future and a hope* (Jeremiah 29:11).

# Surround Yourself with Good People

When I came to New Day Church, I was desperately looking for a place where I felt welcomed and valued. Before I went to church that first time, I prayed that "God would surround me with good people." Marilyn was one of those wonderful people. She always made a beeline over to see me each Sunday. And she would always surprise me by sending lovely, digital cards to my email address. In my difficult life tribulations, she was always checking on me if I needed anything. There were so many times that these difficulties in my life were lessened by Marilyn's kindness to me.

Now she is leaving to move out of state to be with family. This is a good move for her, but I will miss her terribly. Marilyn is a good person whose gentle love and kindness will be missed by everyone at New Day. I know that I will feel sadness at her leaving.

> *In the same way, let your light shine before others, so that they may see your good works and give glory to your Father who is in heaven* (Matthew 5:16).

# My Dog's Life

I adopted my dachshund, Rocky, when he was three years old. He was born with a genetic abnormality in his knees. He doesn't walk like other dogs, but he hops like a rabbit.

I think that Rocky must have been mistreated by a former owner. He is a very timid little guy. He is also afraid of my cane. Instead of using it to walk around the house, I hold on to furniture and walls to get around in order not to scare him. But most of all, Rocky is afraid of men. Whenever a male visits or even a workman comes over to complete a repair of some sort, Rocky hides under the bed and won't move from his spot of safety until the man is gone.

Why would someone ever abuse a sweet, little animal like him? Rocky never does anything wrong. He loves to eat treats, play with my other dachshund, and hops after his red ball. Today, life is good for Rocky. He is content to live with me, and I too am happy that he is an important part of my family.

God watches over his creatures. Whether it is a bird in the air, a serpent slithering across the ground, or even a handicapped little wiener dog, God cares for them all.

*Are not five sparrows sold for two pennies? And not one of them is forgotten before God* (Luke 12:6).

# Losing Your Health

I am a shell of who I used to be. I'm just middle-aged and yet my health isn't good. The MS has robbed me of everything. Sometimes, I get extremely discouraged. I can barely walk, and I can't play the piano anymore. What happened to the young, fit Beth? Who am I if the old me is gone?

I am still the same person inside, and this person isn't perishing. Our physical bodies are just a small part of who we are. God knows what we have accomplished in our lives. He knows what we have tried to do for Him. He also knows when we fail in our endeavors. The body might be weak, but our souls are strong. God knows each of us and won't desert us.

> So we do not lose heart. Though our outer self is wasting away, our inner self is being renewed day by day (2 Corinthians 4:16).

# The Day that My Dad Died

There is something about a parent dying that is unsettling. Never before this time had I felt so lost. I was upset that my dad's body was found on the floor. I don't know why it bothered me so much. The doctor said that his heart attack was immediate and that he was dead before he hit the ground. He was eighty-two years old, so I don't know why I was so troubled. I knew that his death would happen eventually, but I still wasn't ready for it.

I think that in many ways my grief is based on my own selfishness. I am sad because I can't see him anymore. I am also concerned about my multiple sclerosis. If my MS continues to progress and I become very ill, how can I cope with it without my dad? In some ways, I am like a little child who needs her father. We want our parents to be there forever to help provide for us and keep us safe. Regardless of our age, maybe we never stop needing them. I know that I still need my Pops.

*And he called out, "Lord Jesus, receive my spirit"*
(Acts 7:59).

# My MS Has Progressed

I went to purchase a new pair of boots and had a problem. I sat on a stool and repeatedly tried to put a boot on my foot, but I couldn't. My feet were so numb, I couldn't feel them at all. My MS had reached a new level of disability. Finally, when I tried desperately to shove my unresponsive foot into the boot, I fell onto the floor. No one saw it happen, but I was ashamed. How could I continue to function in life if I couldn't even do this small task?

I went home and cried. How could I walk around in the cold if I didn't have boots? Perhaps more importantly, how could I walk around on the ice and snow if I couldn't feel my feet?

So I began to think about the whole concept and asked myself a few difficult questions: *When was the last time that you saw someone with a wheelchair in the snow? Never. You walked with a cane and now use a walker. Do you ever see anyone else walk with a walker in the snow? Absolutely not. How about a cane? No.*

I realized then that other people with walking devices don't get out in the elements either. There is a justified reason why disabled people and the elderly avoid the severe weather.

I knew at that moment that my multiple sclerosis had progressed enough that I had to make a few changes in my life. I would need to make a few accommodations and learn how to ask for assistance from other people. I could still function, but I would need help.

When did I completely lose the feeling in my feet? I don't know, and I suppose it doesn't matter. The important idea to realize is that God loves me, and there are good people in my life who would be more than happy to assist me if I could just tell them that I needed help.

*More than that, we rejoice in our sufferings, knowing that suffering produces endurance, and endurance produces character, and character produces hope, and hope does not put us to shame, because God's love has been poured into our hearts through the Holy Spirit who has been given to us* (Romans 5:3-5).

# Are You an Angel-in-Training?

From what background do angels develop? Maybe they have been here since the beginning of time. Or maybe with the Lord's help, they arise after a terrible illness or life experience. Maybe going through a difficult time helps shape them into someone who can be there for someone else and who understands. In my opinion, this makes sense to me how an angel can be transformed from having a difficult life situation, a tragedy, or a severe illness. I believe that there is a purpose to all of this.

Are you an angel-in-training? Do other people see you as courageous with how you are handling your illness? When you get together with someone, do you spend your time talking about his or her life rather than yourself? Are you a good listener?

Maybe God has a job in mind for you after you leave this life. Maybe the pain and suffering that you are experiencing is helping to form your soul and changing you into a lovely child of God. You could indeed be an angel-in-training. Yes, you could be.

*Do not neglect to show hospitality to strangers, for thereby some have entertained angels unaware* (Hebrews 13:1-2).

# Are You Okay in Heaven, Pops?

The other evening, I said a prayer to my dad. After a year of mourning, I told Pops that I was having a difficult time dealing with his death. I asked him if it was at all possible, if he could somehow tell me that he was okay in heaven.

The next day, I was working very hard at getting my house as clean as possible because an appraiser was coming out so I could refinance. My daughter and her husband came over to help in her bedroom. She was looking through an old pile of college application papers and was getting ready to throw the papers away when something fell out. It was my pop's business card from his old art studio. Clutching the card in her hand, she ran out sobbing from the bedroom. Within a minute, I too was crying. I hadn't seen his old business card in over twenty years and to my knowledge, this card could be the only one that still exists.

Honestly, I didn't expect to hear from my dad. But not only did he tell me that he was okay in heaven, Pops made sure that I knew the message was from him by giving me his business card!

*Blessed are those who mourn, for they shall be comforted* (Matthew 5:4).

# Dealing with Betrayal

I had someone in my life who betrayed me. I was extremely saddened by this treacherous act and for a time, my world-view was warped. But each day, God surrounded me with considerate people. Eventually, through God's love and through the kindness of other individuals, my faith was restored.

Has someone betrayed you? Are you sad each morning when you open your eyes from sleep? Do you fear that no one in the world can be trusted?

May God heal your broken spirit. Do not seek revenge. Instead, live a life of compassion. To help keep your heart strong, pray that the Lord surrounds you with good people to help you recover.

*Do not be overcome by evil, but overcome evil with good* (Romans 12:21).

# Robin Williams Committed Suicide

I was stunned and saddened when Robin Williams committed suicide. I always enjoyed his acting, and knew that when I saw one of his movies I would be in for a treat. I know everyone was in shock that this talented, much loved individual could take his own life.

But depression can be severe and excruciating to those who suffer from it. It can bring agonizing despair that can seem unrelenting.

Are you thinking about committing suicide? God doesn't want you to suffer because He loves you. But things can get better for you. You might not be able to imagine how good your life can be, but God knows the tremendous things that are possible for you. Please know that there is help available. You are a special and adored individual. If you committed suicide, there are people who would be so devastated, they would never recover from it. Pick up the phone now and make that call.

> *I can do all things through him who strengthens me* (Philippians 4:13).

# Feeling Lost

There are numerous meanings for the word, "lost," including something no longer possessed, an item that is missing, or something not won. How about you? Do you feel like a lost sheep? Do you believe that no one would miss you if you vanished from the planet? Do you falsely believe that not even a single person would search for you? Do you sometimes think that your illness or disease makes you a lesser person? Why do you think this?

You are an important person, and the Lord cares for you. If you are lost in your life, God will never stop searching for you. He will never give up until you are found. You always have been and always will be special to Him!

> *What man of you, having a hundred sheep, if he has lost one of them, does not leave the ninety-nine in the open country, and go after the one that is lost, until he finds it* (Luke 15:4)?

# Dark Night of the Soul

"**D**ark Night of the Soul" is a poem written by Saint John of the Cross. According to Wikipedia, it is called the dark night because "darkness represents the hardships and difficulties the soul meets in detachment from the world and reaching the light of the union with the Creator." Many faiths also use this term to describe a spiritual crisis that is marked by profound desolation and fear.

Due to some horrible circumstances in my life, I too experienced my own dark night of the soul. I had a stream of bad things that happened in just a short time period, and I was despondent. I couldn't understand how a God who supposedly loved and cared for me could allow these terrible events to occur. I felt betrayed, abandoned, and grief-stricken. I, who had seen Jesus when I had my near-death experience, even questioned if God actually existed.

Eventually, I realized that God would help me and it was just that He couldn't do it immediately. There were no "quick fixes," and it would take some time before He could alleviate my suffering. The issue wasn't that God didn't care about me. The real problem was the tremendous fear that I was experiencing as well as my impatience.

*When I fall, I shall rise; when I sit in darkness, the Lord will be a light to me* (Micah 7:8).

# Flying the Friendly Skies

About twenty years ago, I was on a flight to go back to see my parents. The plane took off fifty feet in the air and then suddenly dove straight back down to Earth. The passengers screamed, bags fell out of the overhead compartments, and the captain was cursing when his voice quickly came over the announcement to tell us what had happened. Apparently, when we were taking off, another plane had pulled out in our flight path and it was a near miss situation. The plane had blown a tire when we hit the ground, and we had to wait an hour before they could wheel a ladder out so we could leave. With her hat askew on her head, the shaken flight attendant was passing out free miniature bottles of liquor to each guest as we disembarked, and she repeated, "Thank you for flying Delta! Thank you for flying Delta!"

It would have been very easy to never set foot on a plane again. But we had to do so. Until the airline found another flight for us a couple of hours later, I assume that every passenger was worrying about getting back on yet another jet. But we were stranded from where we needed to be.

God is here to provide for you when you are stranded. He will not desert you in your time of need and will help you find the strength to face your fears.

> But they who wait for the Lord shall renew their strength; they shall mount up with wings like eagles; they shall run and not be weary; they shall walk and not faint (Isaiah 40:31).

# Giving to the Poor

My daughter worked part-time at a fast food restaurant. Once when she was at work, two middle-aged men came into the establishment to buy dinner. But the men were not alone; they were accompanied by a third, very thin, disheveled man. When they stood at the counter, they ordered five sandwiches for him, an extra-large fry, and then the homeless man asked for the "biggest milkshake that they had in their store." They then sat down with him as he scarfed down his meal.

The men didn't realize that anyone was watching their quiet deed, but my daughter noticed from behind the counter and will remember their kind deed for the rest of her life.

> *Then the righteous will answer him, saying, "Lord, when did we see you hungry and feed you, or thirsty and give you drink? And when did we see you a stranger and welcome you, or naked and clothe you? And when did we see you sick or in prison and visit you?" And the King will answer them, "Truly, I say to you, as you did it to one of the least of these my brothers, you did it to me"* (Matthew 25:37-40).

# The Horrendous Thunderstorm

We had quite a thunderstorm—lightening flashed excessively, the thunder boomed and crackled, while the rain poured from the sky in buckets. My cats bolted from room to room in terror. My two dogs huddled under the quilt and whined incessantly as if to say, "Please, make it stop." With one large explosion, a lightning bolt hit a tree in the forest behind my home, the wood splintered into the air, and then landed with a crashing sound. All three of my children awoke at the same time and yelled, "Mom!"

As I looked out the window, I answered them, "Everything's alright. We don't need to go to the basement quite yet. I'll let you know if that changes."

We are at the mercy of a thunderstorm. We can't prevent it and have no way to determine the outcome. Just as we have no way to stop nature, there are also hardships in life like having a chronic illness over which we have little control. We pace back and forth to no avail while we lament, "Nothing can be done! What can I do?"

God understands our dismay at life's uncontrollable circumstances. He watches over us and gives us peace during a terrible storm.

> And when he got into the boat, his disciples followed him. And behold, there arose a great storm on the sea, so that the boat was being swamped by the waves; but he was asleep. And they went and woke him, saying, "Save us, Lord; we are perishing." And he said to them, "Why are you afraid, O you of little faith?" Then he rose and rebuked the winds and the

*sea, and there was a great calm. And the men mar-veled saying, "What sort of man is this, that even winds and sea obey him"* (Matthew 8:23-27)*?*

# Skipping, Jumping, Walking

I really can't shop with my daughters anymore. Walking is too difficult and even just a short jaunt would exhaust me. So, they go shopping while I park myself on a bench while I read my newspaper. After I am done catching up on the latest events, I watch people walk.

It is actually fascinating to watch. People all walk very differently. Couples hold hands as they saunter slowly and gaze only at each other. Children jump, skip, and twirl as they hyperactively bolt from item to item. Their mothers follow at a quick pace with one arm outstretched as if to catch their children if they should fall. The elderly shuffle slowly along while their eyes are glued to their feet as if their steady stare would help them successfully navigate each step.

Walking is a tremendous gift from God. It is only after the ability is lost that you realize what you had.

*If we live by the Spirit, let us also walk by the Spirit* (Galatians 5:25).

# The Greatest Gift

I have suffered twenty-four years from multiple sclerosis. Many times, I have asked God, "Why aren't you curing me?" and, "Why won't you take this disease away from me?"

I believe that His reason is twofold. First, He wanted me to write His book on MS. But He didn't ask me to do that major task with any understanding that "If you write this book for me, I'll cure you." You can't make a deal with God. He doesn't work that way. God didn't write the book on MS to help me; He wrote it to help many people who were suffering from the disease. It wouldn't have been fair to the other MS patients for God to pull me aside and say, "Because you are special, I'm going to do this for you." Everyone is special to God. I'm no different, and I don't deserve specialized treatment. If anything were true, it might be whispered that I am one of God's "problem children."

The second reason has to do with why we are here in the first place. In my opinion, our lives are like God's school. He allows us free choice and allows us to experience difficult times for a reason. It would be easier for Him in many ways to just protect us from everything and never allow us to suffer. But a good parent can't do that with their child. Under those circumstances, a child would be so protected, they wouldn't grow as a person. The child would never be able to grow up to be a kind, productive, self-sufficient member of the human race. God wants us to grow and become more "Christ-like" in our behaviors. The only way this can happen is if we experience life and learn from our experiences—bad and good. At the end of our life, He wants to say, "I am proud of you."

In many ways, I think that having MS has been good for me. Before I developed MS, I was arrogant and preoccupied with money and position. Today, these things mean little to me. Through my trials with multiple sclerosis, I have learned never to judge others. There is absolutely no excuse for arrogance in a Christian life, and there was no excuse for my behavior. Through my disease, God has transformed me from a conceited, self-serving woman who thought she was "all that and a bag full of chips" into a better Christian and servant of God. And that might be the greatest gift that He could give to me.

> *For by grace you have been saved through faith. And this is not your own doing; it is the gift of God, not a result of works, so that no one may boast* (Ephesians 2:8-9).

# Trouble Happens in Threes

Have you ever heard the phrase that trouble happens in threes? Sometimes it can seem that way. One misfortune occurs, and you can handle it. A second problem happens, and then things get a little more challenging. But then a third tragedy develops, and you are quickly overwhelmed.

The reality is that we are just human. We are limited in what we are capable of doing. Sometimes we are pushed beyond the limits and everything can seem insurmountable.

I don't think that problems really occur in threes. It's just when we hit that third difficulty, it dawns on us, and we say, "Whew, things have gotten really bad."

God knows that you feel overwhelmed. But regardless of if you just have one problem or even a hundred, the Lord is with you. He has not forgotten your situation and will help you in your time of difficulty.

*This poor man cried, and the Lord heard him and saved him out of all his troubles* (Psalm 34:6).

# Crushed in Spirit

Are you crushed in spirit? Have your problems gone on for so long that you feel they will never end? Is there no possible solution to your terrible situation?

Jesus understands. He also endured a horrendous set of circumstances. He was beaten, spit upon, and nailed to a cross. But that wasn't all. This kind man then hung there for many excruciating hours while people laughed at him and fought over who would get his clothes.

But Jesus knew that there is more beyond this life. He suffered and died so our sins would be forgiven. His gift of sacrifice would put in motion a major transformation of the world's people.

"Why have you forsaken me?" he cried out in despair to God. But the Lord had not forsaken Jesus, and God will not abandon you. He understands that you are suffering, and He hears your pleas. He is standing beside you and leading you by the hand.

*Many are the afflictions of the righteous, but the Lord delivers them all* (Psalm 34:20).

# When Bad Things Happen

W hen Rabbi Harold Kushner's young son was diagnosed with a degenerative disease, Rabbi Kushner searched for answers to the question "why." The answer from this spiritual leader was the best-selling book, *When Bad Things Happen to Good People*. Rabbi Kushner believes in a compassionate God—a God who doesn't make bad things happen to us.

To me, the best example of this philosophy is the story of John Walsh. Known for being a victim rights advocate, Walsh helped develop the longest-running television program *America's Most Wanted* after the murder of his six-year-old son, Adam. AMW aired for twenty-six years and helped capture over a thousand criminals.

God didn't cause this horrible murder, but the Lord helped turn the worst possible tragedy into a new avenue for justice. According to John Walsh, "One missing child is one too many." AMW is Walsh's legacy and a sure sign of God's saving grace when bad things happen.

But there are good things that can happen for a believer even in the darkest of times. With the onset of your disease, life might have changed for you. Maybe like my life with MS, it has changed everything. But, it is what it is.

> *He will wipe away every tear from their eyes, and death shall be no more, neither shall there be mourning, nor crying, nor pain, for the former things have passed away* (Revelation 21:4).

# Suffering Is Just a Moment in Time

My MS continues to attack me, no matter what the doctors do to stop it. Every day, I lose a little bit more of who I used to be. During one very depressed moment, it seemed to me like I was just waiting to die.

Although it might appear that I am just a shell of the person that I used to be, God knows who I am and what I have tried to accomplish in my life. He knows about my numerous failures and the times that I have succeeded in my endeavors. He also is very aware that my MS is rapidly progressing. God hears my cries and knows that I am afraid of what is coming next. But I'm not dead yet. Maybe there is more that God wants me to do. In my mind, this is the only explanation for why I am still here.

Jesus too was terrified of what was happening to him. He cried out to God, "Why have you forsaken me?" But God had not abandoned Jesus. The suffering that Jesus experienced was a necessary part in God's grand plan to change the world.

Today, I will look beyond my current situation. I will turn my fears over to God, because my suffering is just a moment in time and a moment does not a lifetime make. Instead, I will ask God to show me how I can use the rest of my life to help Him.

*For this light momentary affliction is preparing for us an eternal weight of glory beyond all comparison* (2 Corinthians 4:17).

# Air in the Tires

It was a snowy, icy day. I didn't want to go out, but I had to drive to a doctor's appointment. I stopped first to get gas in my car. When I went inside the station, an elderly woman was asking the attendant for something. "Could you help put air in my tires?"

"Oh no, I am here by myself and can't leave the booth unattended," the worker told her. Numerous thoughts quickly went racing through my head. *The air pump is on the opposite side of the parking lot, and it's slippery. I have no business doing this, I'm handicapped.* Next, I don't know if it was Jesus who then spoke to me or if it was in fact the distant sound of my mother putting the fear of God in my head, but a voice loudly said in my mind, "Get your buns over there!" My eyes popped wide open in surprise, and I quickly turned to the woman. "I'll help you."

The elderly woman and I inched our way across the parking lot to the air pump. I showed her how to remove the little cap and put it in a safe location. I then demonstrated how to hold the handle firmly in place and squeeze it while the air was inserted. I also explained to her how to determine how much air was needed.

As we were completing the task, she thanked me. "My husband always did this for me."

Without thinking, I quickly blurted out, "Where is he today?"

Her eyes then filled with tears as she replied, "He's in the funeral home. That's where I'm going next."

My mouth dropped open in shock, "I am so sorry. Can I give you a hug?" We then embraced for a long period of time. As we parted ways, I told her, "Well, now you know how to put air in the tires. You are going to be okay."

*So whoever knows the right thing to do and fails to do it, for him it is sin* (James 4:17).

# Dying Earlier than Most

My doctor tells me that my MS will eventually kill me. In all honesty, this is really not news to me. I have suspected for quite some time that this would be how my disease would end, but to actually hear these words from my doctor was shocking. I then asked her how many years she thought that I had left. She wasn't sure, but she concluded by saying, "The MS is attacking your brain and causing it to resemble swiss cheese. You can't live for long with a brain that resembles a food product. You will not live to see old age."

I'm not so sure that she is right. The truth about dying is that none of us know how long we have. A perfectly healthy person can be walking along and suddenly drop dead. Then, there are others who beat the odds and live for decades with cancer.

Whether you are going to live a long life, or whether you will die earlier than most, is immaterial. We all die. It is not how long you have that is important, it is what you do with that time that makes your life worthwhile.

*So teach us to number our days that we may get a heart of wisdom* (Psalm 90:12).

# Skin Color, Eye Color, Hair Color

I am blind to the color of a person's skin. Race is irrelevant to me. I might notice it when I first meet someone. In order to recognize her when I see her again, I might note that she is taller than me, displays her happiness with a loud explosive laugh, and has lovely caramel-colored skin. But it doesn't register with me after that first meeting.

My daughter was having a play-date with a new schoolmate. The mother was planning on stopping by to pick her up. In the meantime, I was having coffee with my friend. She and I had been pals for years and were sharing our current experiences with each other.

The mother arrived to pick up her daughter. My friend was just leaving, but I introduced them as she headed out the door.

Then the mother said, "I didn't know that you had any black friends."

I responded with surprise, "Who?"

The mother seemed shocked at my response and answered me, "That lady who just left!"

I was silent for a moment and then said, "Was she black? I didn't notice." Needless to say, that was the last time my daughter's friend was over for a play-date.

All of God's creatures are different. A zebra's stripes are as unique as fingerprints. Enormous coconut crabs are sixteen inches long and weigh nine pounds. A starfish has two stomachs, but doesn't have a brain. Why would God go to so much trouble? Couldn't God just save Himself some work by skipping on a few tasks? Wouldn't it be easier for Him if all snowflakes were the same?

God in His infinite wisdom loves variety. Viva la différence!

*So Peter opened his mouth and said: "Truly, I understand that God shows no partiality"* (Acts 10:34).

# Broken People

Physically, I am a broken person because of my multiple sclerosis and because I am a victim of domestic violence. That's the way it is. There's no denying it. Spiritually, though, I'm a rock. That's true too.

Sometimes I think about why all of these terrible things have happened to me. A few bad choices, but in most cases, they were not my fault. I think about the "whys," but I don't know why really. I've been through it—abuse, disease, pain. Maybe the question isn't really "why," but "how." How has going through these things changed me?

To start with, I try very hard never to judge others. I feel that I have no right to do so. I understand in ways that very few people can. I have numerous friends—doctors, lawyers, teachers, business people, an alcoholic, a gambling addict, a homeless man, and a former prostitute who was trafficked as a child. I don't judge them in any way, shape, or form. They are all special and lovely to me.

Material things mean nothing to me anymore either—not clothes, money, or possessions. Things can be gone in the blink of an eye and really mean little. What is important to me are friendships, my animals, nature, my boyfriend, and my family. Out of all these things, though, God means the most to me. He is truly my best friend. My life has little meaning without Him.

People can sit around feeling sorry for themselves and complaining about their lives. I've done my share. But it didn't help anything and just wasted time.

Abuse? Uh-huh. Disease, pain, despair, fear, sadness—big time. But really, these experiences are now irrelevant. What is important is what I have learned and who I am now through the help of Jesus.

It's not over yet, but I'm not afraid. God helps broken people. Maybe, the best is yet to come.

> *The Lord is near to the brokenhearted and saves the crushed in spirit* (Psalm 34:18).

# In Conclusion

This is the end of *So You Have a Disease: Devotions and Stories to Restore Hope.* The book is out of my head now, and I can rest.

I hope that this book has been of some help to you.

If you are suffering from a chronic illness or disease, you will have good days and difficult days with your struggle. But you are more than your disease. You are a mother, father, friend, husband, wife, employee, boss, and teacher. You are so much more.

Remember, science is progressing. They are finding new cures and treatments every day. Perhaps they will find a cure for your illness soon. Or perhaps it will take many lifetimes before they do. But there is more after this life. We are here for a reason—to learn as much as we can, to love with the whole of our being, and to serve God with every breath in our bodies. No matter how ill you are, no matter how broken your body is, you are important. You are special in God's eyes. You are not alone.

Live your life with happiness, joy, and peace. God bless you, my lovely friend.

Printed in the United States
By Bookmasters